A PERSONAL DISCOVERY CAREER GUIDE & WORKBOOK

NOW WHAT?

109+ Questions For Uncovering Your Life's Purpose, Passion & Place

For Those Who Are Side Hustling, Career Building, or Just Fed Up!

BY

ANGIE VANARSDALE

Aren't you glad you read all this fun stuff?

This book is dedicated to the most loving and courageous person in my life.

Audra, I am so proud of you! It took courage to start over, to reinvent yourself. That one

decision, to follow your dreams, will forever change the lives of everyone you touch.

I will be eternally grateful that you have touched and changed mine.

Alex and Yoli, thank you for your continuous love and support.

You're the best friends a person could ask for!

MMA, thank you for the push—Phoenix rising!

To my writing buddies: Bella and Luna

CONTENTS

WELCOME!

Hello my friend! I am grateful you are here.

I wish I knew the path you have taken to get to this place, but despite not having met you, there's one thing I know for sure; your arrival is not an accident, it's by design! So, grab a cup of coffee, put your feet up and make yourself uncomfortable (oh I mean comfortable) and if you are listening in the car, please, just keep your eyes on the road and hands solidly on the wheel. Let's do this!

Oh, and I have a special favor to ask: If this book is valuable to you, I'd sincerely appreciate it if you could share your honest feedback. It doesn't take much, just a couple of sentences, but the time you give helps others find this book perhaps when they need it most.

A THANK YOU GIFT!

Because you picked up NOW WHAT, you've unlocked something powerful, a **free course** that helps you discover the intersection of what you love, what you're good at, what the world needs, and what you can get paid for. It's your next move toward clarity, confidence, and a life that actually fits you. Thank you again!

THE CALL

It was a cloudy fall day, I had just gotten a cup of coffee and sat down at a table in anticipation of meeting a potential coaching client. In the door walked a smartly dressed woman bearing an air of confidence and a look of authority that said, "Hello world! I've got you." I was sincerely surprised when she walked up to me and asked, "Are you Angie?"

Her story, like countless others I have had the privilege of listening to, was an all-too familiar one. She felt overwhelmed, trapped, used, beaten down, defeated (I could go on, but you get the hole she believed she was in).

The title she had chased and contentedly attached to her name plate now felt like a one-thousand -pound gold chain wrapped around her neck. Her degree abbreviations were formless letters following the name of a person she no longer recognized. The work to achieve financial freedom and chase fulfillment ended up being a shape shifter; a dream turned into gilded handcuffs. No money nor incentive package could buy back time or make up for the life she felt she'd lost. Exhaustion, disappointment, anger, despair were the forgettable fruits of her 60+ hour a week labors for over 15 years.

By the time she sat down to have coffee with me, she was done. The stick a fork in me, kind of done. Who am I? What is my life about now? Where do I go from here? Tears welled up in her eyes as I could see those questions stare blankly back at her with no answers to offer. There was no escaping it, she needed answers, an exit strategy, and a solid picture of a new future and fast. "Hope for two please," I almost shouted to the barista.

Her experience may be different from yours, but here's my hunch, if you purchased this book, you might be itching to do something different or desire to discover and uncover a more meaningful life. You are an answer seeker, that like many of us at one time or another, feel stuck.

- Is your work a vampire, slowly sucking the life out of you, leaving you feeling exhausted, hopeless, unfulfilled, and trapped?

- Perhaps you are content with everything in your life, but there is still that nagging voice that calls to you: "C'mon! Let's do something new!"

- Are you stuck in a situation you should walk away from but don't seem to have the strength to find the door?

- Have you ever quit your job ("hell yes I'm leaving") because you were flat out fed up only to leave and then freak out, "Oh, no! Now what?"

- Are you THAT person, yes you, the one that can talk yourself into or out of anything? "It's not that bad. It could be worse. At least I have a job, even though I dislike it most of the time."

- Do your weekends play out this way? Saturday you're feeling great! Then Sunday afternoon hits, and suddenly, that happiness begins to shrink into a pile of apprehension and dread as the clock ticks down the minutes to mondain Monday.

The hard truth: situations like these fit all shapes and sizes and come with warning signs (boredom, exhaustion, frustration, anger, anxiety, stress) and natural consequences if one fails to truly pay attention.

My friends, it's time to step off the proverbial hamster wheel! Whatever your current situation, you are being called to move, break free from the familiar, say goodbye to the status quo, do something different. YOUR kind of different. Regardless of the catalyst: heartbreak, frustration, boredom, a crazy boss, the little voice inside your head that simply won't shut the hell up or what I affectionately call the itch to switch, you have in your hands a step-by-step coaching guide with essential questions that will help you begin to navigate and map out the course of your personal career and life's journey. It's time to start asking and begin answering. You've got this! Living your best life starts today and my friends it's long overdue!

THE POWER OF QUESTIONS

It's a fundamental truth: the quality of the questions we ask ourselves determines what we think about, what options we consider, the direction we choose to go and ultimately the results we achieve. Successful people ask questions others don't. Questions, and most importantly, the answers, are the key to changing the course of anything in your life. If supercharging your dreams and taking control of your future was the motive for picking up this book, then let's get started!

A Personal Coach in Your Pocket

Congratulations, you now have a personal life coach in your pocket! This is a book of questions designed to help you decipher and identify your true north. After answering these questions, your values, goals, and desires will be lit up like a Christmas tree. Once you figure out what you're willing to stand for, what you want and why you want it, the hows involved in making it happen becomes clearer. The path is set.

The goal of this book is for you to feel the power and hope of being in the driver's seat of your life, hands firmly on the steering wheel with your foot on the gas. As your coach, I am not going to apologize for pushing you. You are here because you are a seeker, a believer, and a doer. What this journey requires of you is honesty. That means no B.S. or well maybes, or I'll tries, you hear! The more honest you are with yourself the more you take away from this experience. Don't worry, I'm not going to look over your shoulder or grab you through the pages (that's creepy).

If you need others to help you stay accountable or just don't want to do this alone, then join an amazing community of seekers just like you. Our __Thrive Tribe__ Facebook community is exclusively for owners and operators of this book. There you can find bonus material, inspiration, articles, and even more life-changing questions as well as a community of like-minded individuals to keep you going and inspired. I will be there cheering you on as well!

Before You Begin

Questions start off simple and pick up in intensity. You might be able to answer the warmup questions easily without doing many mental calisthenics, but others might require a bit more consideration, rumination, marinating, and processing.

There are over 110 questions so unless you are an overachiever and want to finish them all in one sitting, it's best to complete this in a week's time. Try not to rush through it. It is not a speed test nor a race to see who can finish first, it's an investment in you. You will know you have done well if you read over your responses and can say, "yes, that answer feels right to me."

I know it seems simple enough, the answering of questions, but there will be times when this mental workout will leave you tired. Don't worry, it's part of the process. Trust me, the time and tiredness will be worth the effort.

The questions are divided into numbered sessions. Complete the sessions how you choose. You can:

1. tackle one session at a time.

2. go about it numerically, taking the odd numbered questions first and then finish up with the even numbered questions.

3. jump around answering only those questions that interest you in the moment.

4. start with the easy questions at the top of each session and work your way through to the more thought-provoking ones.

Your approach doesn't matter. Answering most if not all the questions does matter. Some questions may sound repetitive, but each is designed to bring into clearer and clearer focus the picture of the life that's waiting for you.

A downloadable copy of the workbook is available for free on the Facebook page. If you have the workbook, you can check off each question as you complete it. There is also space to write your answers as well as "HMMM" pages should you need more space to write answers, reflections or simply doodle. Whether you have the workbook or are using any piece of paper

10

you can find, it is helpful to keep your answers, notes, and responses in one place as a reference. Your responses are your personal breadcrumbs helping lead you back to yourself should you get lost along the way.

I love rereading my answers and periodically, asking myself the questions again. I use it as a grounding and recentering exercise. Answers act as gentle reminders of what I care most about and what's important for me to focus on and give attention to, especially when life gets crazy, or I start having doubts about my direction or purpose. This is something you can keep coming back to, like a permanent home base.

"The quality of your life is determined by the quality of questions you ask yourself. "

---me

MASTERING YOUR MINDSET: SETTING THE TABLE

I see it in your eyes, you may be tempted to skip this mindset stuff and head straight for the questions. That's fine. I get it, but don't say I didn't warn you! Stretching and warming up is key to any successful exercise routine. Setting your intentions and mindset for these exercises is no different. Anyone can answer questions, but those that set clear intentions of having an open and inquisitive mind get the most from this experience. If you come in closed off, unconsciously hurrying through the questions with little thought or consideration, the answers will provide little insight. This book is designed to help you dig. Expect that at times you will be uncomfortable and working some mental muscles! Part of your journey through this experience is to get comfortable being uncomfortable. Growth and wisdom are often found in uncomfortable spaces.

If you possess a mindfulness practice or routine that helps anchor you in the present, make sure to engage in it. Whether it's meditation, prayer, sitting quietly, or going for a walk, the specific activity doesn't matter. Personally, I find that exercising before tackling my tasks is particularly effective in focusing my thoughts and calming my mind.

If this centering stuff is foreign to you, no problem! Find a location where you can relax, free from anything that may distract you from concentrating on your answers. The goal is to put yourself in an environment where you can hear yourself think, so find that best thinking space for you.

When you are comfortable, it's time to "set the table". Setting the table simply means clearing your mind and preparing a space where your heart, head and gut can show up to answer questions authentically. No ego fake talk here please!

Mantras are a great way to prepare your mind and set the intention for your Q&A session. Here are a couple to try on:

- I am honestly and humbly answering these questions today to unlock the truths of my happiness and purist wishes.

- I gain clarity of who I am and what I want with each question I answer.

- The answers I have around my life's longings are waiting to be uncovered!

- I come with an open mind and a questioning nature. Show me the way!

- Today, I am investing in me and reinventing my future!

CAUTION: NOTE TO SELF

To the perfectionist, there are no right or wrong answers, just your answers (don't get all judgy/judgy on yourself)!

To those of you serial thinkers, try not to overthink things. There's no need to over process this stuff. Go with your gut, trust your intuition, and get on getting on.

To those of you who insist on answering a question by first asking, "what will others think?" Remember, no one else is going to read this except you. Besides, this work isn't for anyone else. Please stay far away from Shouldville, answering questions about how you think others would like you to answer them.

For those of you folks that can't wait to answer the questions and get to the end of the book, set a goal to complete each session and challenge yourself to take time and care in providing the most thoughtful answers. Quality over speed my friends.

Now that you are in your perfect headspace, let's begin! Each session of questions purposefully starts without explanation or definition. All will become clear at the end, I promise. The questions and your answers await. Good luck! I will see you on the other side.

SESSION 1

1. What were you obsessed with when you were a kid?

2. What were your favorite things to do in the past?

3. What about now?

4. What did your 15-year-old self-imagine you'd be doing right now?

5. What is at the top of your bucket list and why?

6. What's something about yourself or your life that might surprise others to learn?

7. What's a quote that inspires you and why?

8. What's the best gift anyone's ever given you? Why was it "the best"?

9. What kind of life roles do you enjoy living?

SESSION 2

10. What's been the most satisfying thing you have ever done?

11. If you were asked to write a book, what would it be about?

12. What could you talk to someone about for hours and never get bored?

13. If you had to leave your house all day, every day, but it wasn't to go to your current job, where would you go and what would you do?

14. What activities are you doing when time flies and the world around you goes unnoticed?

15. What have you done that you love to spend time on? Why?

16. What's something you'll spend time doing, no matter what?

17. If you didn't have to sleep, what would you do with the extra time?

18. What do you wish you had more time to do?

19. What would you build if you had unlimited resources?

20. What have you done that made you the proudest?

SESSION 3

Strong work! Keep it up!

21. What specifically would you like to experience in life?

22. What chapters would you separate your autobiography into?

23. What's been the most meaningful life experience you've gone through?

24. Why was it the most meaningful?

25. What places or events have transformed your ideas, thinking, perspective, or made you feel alive?

26. What life experiences have shaped your personality and character in the most profound way?

"If the light is in your heart, you will find your way home."

---Rumi

SESSION 4

You are humming now!

27. What verb best describes you?

28. You're in an elevator with your hero. You have 90 seconds to tell them about yourself. What do you say?

29. What's memorable about you?

30. If you could be a different person, who would you be? Why?

31. What do you secretly love about yourself?

32. What do you struggle the most with in life?

33. What do people come to you for?

34. What do other people always thank you for?

35. What do others say you are meant to do with your life?

36. In what situations are you the most confident?

SESSION 5

37. A stylist notices a complicated hairstyle, a singer notices a talented vocalist... what do you notice?

38. What are you drawn to (can be anything—art, music, movies, books, crafts)?

39. What kind of "shower ideas" do you get?

40. Over the last 6 months, when have you felt the most alive and electrified?

41. Who inspires you most? (Anyone you know or do not know. Family, friends, authors, artists, leaders, etc.)

42. Which qualities do these people possess that you find attractive or inspiring?

43. What's your theme song? Why?

44. If you could invent something, what would you invent (even if it's not real, like a time machine or a magic wand)?

45. If you could follow someone around for a day, who would you follow around and why?

SESSION 6

46. What makes you smile?

47. When was the last time you felt "lit up"?

48. What is your favorite inspirational movie and why do you find it inspiring?

49. Where do you find the most inspiration?

50. What makes you feel great about yourself?

51. If you could choose your feelings which feelings, would you like to experience most of the time? Why?

52. What gives you strength or makes you feel strong?

53. When do you feel the most confident about yourself?

54. What do you do to get your energy back, "fill up" the energy bucket after a long week or situation that leaves you feeling drained?

55. When do you feel the most like yourself? What situations are you most often in when you feel this way?

56. How would a good friend describe you when you are at your best?

SESSION 7

57. What is the most important trait you possess that you hold dear?

58. What are the traits or values you most admire in others?

59. What do others do that feels unfair?

60. If you could get a message across to a large group of people. Who would those people be? What would your message be?

61. What do you stand up for?

62. What do you stand against?

63. What values guide your actions?

64. What fears freeze you most often?

65. What fears move you to action?

"Let yourself be silently drawn by the strange pull of what you love. It will not lead you astray."

---Rumi

SESSION 8

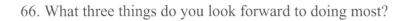

66. What three things do you look forward to doing most?

67. What activities make you feel fully alive and invigorated?

68. What would you do if you could not fail?

69. If you had to go back to school, what would you go back to school to study? Why?

70. What things do you love to create/develop?

71. If you had to teach something, what would you teach?

72. Walk around your home. What items do you love? Why?

73. What's something you'd do even if you never made any money?

74. What dreams would you pursue if you had unlimited potential?

75. What do you love reading or hearing about?

76. What problems do you love to solve?

77. What could you give for a 40-minute presentation with absolutely no preparation?

78. How do you typically express your own version of creativity?

79. What's a job you'd never want to do? Why?

SESSION 9

80. How do you feel you should spend your time?

81. If you have a job, why are you working where you are now?

82. What are three things you do because others think you should?

83. What would you do if no one needed a/an [insert your job role here] anymore?

84. If you are in school, why are you studying what you are studying?

85. What life roles you have now just don't suit you or you've outgrown?

86. Where do you spend most of your time because you think you should?

87. What would you do if you didn't care what others thought?

88. What do you do every day because you worry about what others will think of you?

89. How do you think others should approach you (think communication wise)?

90. What expectations do you have of others that you also have for yourself?

SESSION 10

91. Which of your traits and attributes seem to stand out most?

92. What key skills/knowledge/abilities are of most value to you? To others?

93. What abilities do you have that are unique and distinct from other people?

94. What would you describe as your natural talents and abilities?

95. What are your three key weaknesses?

1.

2.

3.

96. How do your strengths/knowledge/abilities connect to what I love?

SESSION 11

97. How would you like to make a difference to others?

98. What causes are you the most excited about?

99. How do you tend to help others who need you?

100.   What kinds of people do you like to be around and help?

101.   Where could you provide the most value to others?

102.   How would you like to impact the world?

103.   What problem do you care about that's larger than you?

104. What individuals or groups do you identify the most with?

105. How have your difficulties equipped you to serve others?

106. What legacy would you like to leave?

107. How will the world be a better place because you have lived?

108. Given what you know about yourself, what effort is calling you to move?

109. You're given one wish, but you can't use it on yourself. What would you wish for?

WELCOME BACK!

    Look at you! Strong Work! You killed it! How do you feel?   Now let's look at what we can uncover through your answers.

SURPRISE!!!

Do you like surprises? Of course you do! As a way of saying thank you for working through all the questions I have a special gift just for you! Make sure to check it out at the end of the book. (If you can't wait till the end, it's on page 117!)

"There is a candle in your heart, ready to be kindled. There is a void in your soul, ready to be filled. You feel it, don't you?"

----Rumi

MASTERS EXERCISE 1: FIRST THINGS FIRST

Before jumping into the various exercises, let's pause and briefly take a moment to check out your beautiful work and responses! As quickly as you can, jot down any initial aha's, surprises, pauses, thought-provoking questions or anything that caught your attention as you were responding to the questions.

What did you notice?

MASTERS EXERCISE 2: A CLOSER LOOK

Each session's answers provide you with the all-important clues, answers, direction, and feedback you need to identify a rewarding job, profession, hobby, work, or life path. Pay close attention as we work one session of questions at a time. This process will be the same for each session's question set.

Your goal in this exercise is to identify patterns in your answers. Later, you will amplify these discoveries to focus on what is most important and sacred to you.

Step 1: Review your answers in Session One. Taking a set of highlighters or a pen, go back through your answers and highlight or draw a circle around those words, ideas or concepts that are similar to or like one another. If you played Memory as a child, this is a grown-up version!

As an example, for session one, maybe you were obsessed with racing go-carts as a kid. Your bucket list includes a trip to see a Nascar or a National Drag Racing event. Your favorite quote might be "Just Do It".

These words would be highlighted, circled, or underlined as in this example, because they have things in common. What do you think go-cart racing, Nascar, Drag Racing and Just Do It have in common? They represent an action-orientation, movement, physical energy, speed, adrenaline, excitement, expediency, urgency, self-control, direction, a challenge. Your goal is to look for possible and meaningful connections and group them together. Have fun with this!

Step 2: Continue grouping things together. Some answers may be a part of various groupings. Using the previous example, go-cart racing, Nascar and Drag Racing could all be in a group that later could be labeled as "Racing". There are no correct number of groups. If you find quite a few, consider using different markers or colors to distinguish connected answers from one another. This will make identifying and labeling them easier.

Step 3: After you have exhausted identifying commonalities for that session, label or give the session a name or descriptive word or words that summarize the common characteristics.

Don't overthink it. This isn't a test, just give it a name or label. I labeled the session above: Action.

Step 4: Follow Steps 1-3 for each session.

Step 5: Write the name or labels you've given each session in the corresponding session circle.

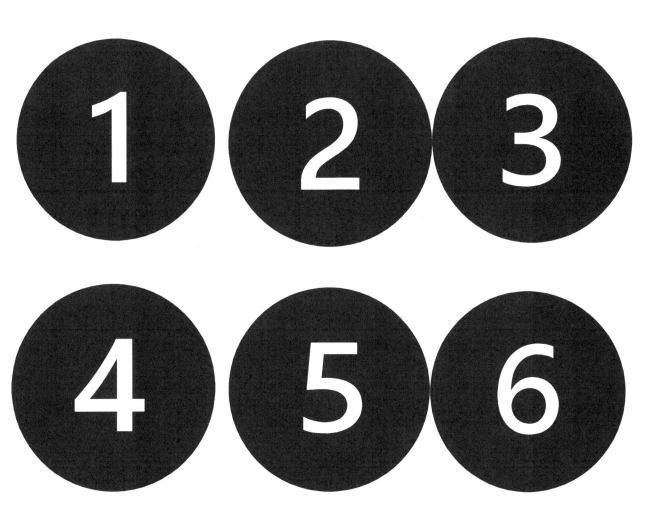

7

8

9

10

1☐

Step 6: Answer the following questions:

Do you see similar words or topic patterns amongst the labels/category descriptions across all your circles?

If so, what are they?

Are there significant differences in your labels or categories?

You may or may not start seeing larger patterns surfacing. If you do, pay attention because these are spotlights of interest that are clearly important to you.

MASTERS EXERCISE 3: FOCUSING IN

Answering the questions and reviewing your responses is a fun exercise, but if I know you, it's about how this information aids in planning and guiding your life. Let's look at your answers in each Session and begin to unpack how they directly apply to designing the life you desire.

Session and Circle One: Warmup

The first session was a warmup that included questions like those in later sessions. In working with clients, the practice of reviewing and getting reconnected or reacquainted with past hobbies or interests often provides clues of interests and passions that still hold a spark.

Review your answers in Session 1 and your first circle and then answer these important questions:

Do you see any past interests that still hold interest for you today? If so, what are they?

Are there activities from past interests which you still enjoy or wish you could spend more time doing?

How might you incorporate the joy of these activities or passions in your life today?

Session and Circle Two: Loves

Clearly, no one wants to spend the rest of their lives doing something they dislike or worse yet hate, yet we've all probably done it. Often, I see people foregoing the love of work for work that pays the mortgage or keeps the world seemingly safe and sound. The devil we know is often perceived as better than the devilish unknown. There is no judgement here.

As you rethink your aspirations for the future, this session will help identify what truly captivates you. It's crucial to keep in mind the things that consistently bring you joy. The better we understand our passions, what excites us, and why we find these pursuits fulfilling, the more we can purposefully weave them into our daily routines and professional endeavors.

After reviewing your answers, here are additional questions you may find helpful:

What captivates me the most about the activities or pursuits I claim to love or feel passionate about? In other words, what draws me to love these things so deeply? What benefits or satisfaction do they offer me?

Where does what I love already exist in my life?

What could I stop doing to make room for what I love to do?

Is there any way I can increase the amount of time I spend doing what I love or find joy in, while minimizing what I have little interest in spending time on?

To give you a short personal example, I love building virtually anything and can spend countless hours transforming or refurbing something old and giving it a new look or purpose. This says a lot about me. I need to build and create and get pure joy from seeing the results of my efforts. I tangibly must make something better. This need inspired me to write this book, a physical and tangible object designed to help transform or reinvent lives.

Session and Circle Three: Experiences

Life should be fully experienced, not just passively existed in, hurried through, or captured solely for the sake of social media appearances. Considering we spend a significant portion of our lives working and life is fundamentally about experiences, what kind of experiences do you wish to accumulate throughout your career? What experiences could new work or reframing current work afford you? If you discovered your dream job, one that aligns perfectly with your life's goals, how would that transform your experience of life and your perspective on the world?

I was hired by a client who by all definitions was wildly successful. Most everything in his life was going well with one exception, he was becoming more incensed about recently being passed over for promotions he felt he deserved. He would apply and get rejected, apply, and get turned down and before long his internal frustration had reached the boiling point, and his self-confidence was visibly shaken. His irritation was evident to all who had the unfortunate experience of collaborating and working with him; his increasingly snappy demeanor exacerbated the situation and strained his relationships, further complicating his path to achieving his goals. By the time we sat down for a discussion, the situation had escalated significantly to the point of eruption.

From the outset of our sessions, it became evident that despite his lifelong pursuit and attainment of job titles, he remained profoundly dissatisfied with his career. He had always equated success with promotions and upward mobility, but now, facing obstacles in his advancement, his previously subdued sense of lack of fulfillment internally had manifested itself externally.

During our time working together, he came to understand that his deepest desire was for a variety of dynamic and ever-changing life and work experiences—chances to grow, learn, leverage his abilities, and constantly redefine himself. I encouraged him to clearly define and map out the kinds of experiences he was seeking and then begin to look for job openings that he thought could provide and afford him those specific opportunities. The goal of the job search was no longer simply about chasing a job title or pay, it was about making a career choice that supported him in experiencing life the way he wished and deserved. As our sessions concluded, he recognized he had the opportunity to attain the experiences he desired by reassessing and reframing the job he currently had. His current salary and positional tenure provided him with the financial resources and flexibility of time to pursue experiences outside his job. He also discovered projects he could volunteer to lead within his current role that would help him grow in his areas of interest.

Frequently, addressing feelings of unhappiness and dissatisfaction doesn't necessitate changing jobs; instead, it might be enough to adjust your perspective on your current role and the opportunities it presents. By taking a moment to consider how you can alter your approach or mindset and reminding yourself of the reasons why you made this career choice, you may find the fulfillment you're seeking.

What do you desire to experience in all aspects of your life? (e.g., Occupation, Family, Friends, Finances, Home, Spiritually, Physically, Mentally) Take some time with this one, it's important!

What actions could you take to create the experiences you desire to have? What could you do today, tomorrow, or in the upcoming weeks to move towards creating or acquiring those experiences?

What type of work environment do you want to experience? How would you know it if you saw it? How would it feel or look? How would you describe its characteristics?

The best experiences (work, life, home, relationship/friendship, travel) of my life have been:

They were/are meaningful to me because:

I would like to experience   my life and can do that by:

A couple of examples:

I want to experience being able to get up every morning and leisurely start my day without a stressful commute. I can do that by finding a position where I am allowed to telecommute to work and set my own schedule.

I want to experience a sense of community and camaraderie in a supportive work atmosphere. I can do that by finding someone I can personally support on my team. I can ask questions about the team environment in my interview.

I want to experience work where I feel I am making a difference, and that difference is appreciated. I can do that by volunteering my time to a non-profit that needs my unique skill set.

I want to experience enjoying tapas and red wine in Spain. I will do that by planning a trip to Spain by finding a tour company and begin saving money to visit.

Be precise about the experiences you seek. The clearer you are in articulating your desired experiences, the more focused and proactive you'll be in spotting and seizing opportunities when they present themselves. An important tip: while outlining what you wish to experience, avoid fixating on the specific ways in which the experiences might happen. Aim for a wide range of possibilities. There are an infinite number of paths you could take for experiences to manifest themselves in your life. There is magic in the synchronicities that present themselves when you are clear about the "what" but remain open and unattached to the "how".

To conclude this session, it's important to recognize we all do things or desire to acquire things in our lives because we want to experience something or avoid experiencing something. Beginning your career and life planning with a clear understanding of what you genuinely wish to experience in your lifetime is crucial. This clarity is a foundational step in setting priorities that determine what opportunities you say yes and no to.

Session and Circle Four: Your Special Sauce

In a world where people want to stand out it's surprising how many of us work so hard to fit in and be just like everyone else. We forget that our uniqueness is a download, a gift that only we have received. The person you are and are always becoming will never exist on this planet again, ever. Like NEVER! These session's questions uncover what you and usually others see as your uniqueness.

As you review your answers ask yourself these questions:

How can these gifts find expression in my current work?

Could I start a side hustle or make money doing something people usually ask me to help with?

How might people pay me to solve problems that I naturally and easily solve?

Session and Circle Five: Attention Please!

If I asked you to notice all the white vehicles on the road you may find while you are driving tomorrow or the next day, noticing more white vehicles than say red ones. What's interesting is our brain filters out a lot of what we see, hear, and experience based on what's important to us, what resonates with our view of the world. As you look at your answers in this session:

What are you paying the most attention to?

What do you find inspires you?

What gets your attention on a regular basis?

What do you notice that others don't?

What desires keep tugging at your heart that you can't help but pay attention to?

Ironically paying attention to what grabs your attention gets you closer to knowing what you love, care about or are passionate about. This may seem obvious but it's worth repeating; you pay little attention to things you are not interested in!

Session and Circle Six: Feelings

Let's face it, we all want to feel a certain way or not feel other ways and we do the things we do to obtain the feelings we like and love and run in the other direction to avoid those we don't. If we are honest about chasing feelings, then it is wickedly important to have clarity on what we want to catch. In reviewing your answers in this session:

What do you want to feel (at least most of the time) or not feel.

What do your answers tell you about how you would like to feel on a regular basis?

Could you feel that way now without changing anything in your life?

What would need to change for you to feel more of what you desire to feel?

How do you want to make others feel in your presence?

Session and Circle Seven: Values and Fears

The heart of the pandemic was what I call The Big Reflector or The Call. For millions of people, this singular event was a wakeup call of seismic proportion, a mirror reflecting and illuminating what was valued, feared, and needed most in life.

Many of us went from racing a thousand miles an hour to a heart wrenching halt, poignant pause, or a flat-out jarring stop as we tried to find our way through the new chaotic energy desiring a level of control, security, and balance.

This unraveling of our ordinary lives created an extraordinary opportunity to pause, realign, reinvent, become resourceful, resign, reflect, reframe, and refine what we wanted, what we didn't want, and what needed to be different in our lives. Covid became a catalyst to question: Is this the work I really want to do? Does this organization really care about me? What am I willing or not willing to give to this job? Am I doing meaningful work? Do I care enough to stay? How do I create a sense of balance in my life and where do I draw the line? What type of work environment do I desire for myself? What is my time worth? Is this worth my time?

You might be experiencing some of these questions yourself. The goal of this session is to clarify what you value and care most about by analyzing your answers and asking these follow up questions:

Am I living these values?

Are my values finding expression in my life? In other words, am I living my values?

Does my work align with my values? If not, why not?

I also asked you to answer a few questions about the elephant in most people's rooms: fears. You and I could spend an entire day talking about fears and how to manage them, but here are some simple truths about fear:

- What you desire is just on the other side of what you think you fear.

- You only need to focus on taking the next logical step to keep fear in its place for the moment.

- The closer you get to realizing your dreams the more fear wants to rear its ugly head.

- Fear isn't always your enemy!

If you and I get the chance to work together in a future masterclass workshop we will identify your individual fear profile and help you develop a plan for working with it, through it, avoiding being paralyzed by it. In the meantime, here are some helpful questions:

What scares you as it relates to becoming the best version of yourself?

How is fear impacting your decisions to do something or not do something you care about?

What do you value so much that the desire for it never goes away?

I value:

This value (these values) is (are) important to me because:

I desire to express these values in/by:

This is what I personally value most about myself:

Session and Circle Eight: Enjoyment

I'm hoping you gave yourself permission to have some fun with the questions in this session. There is joy and hope in possibility. Love it and live it baby! (My version of ride or die)

What brings you joy?

What struggles are you willing to endure to discover joy?

Can you find joy in the journey you are on rather than waiting for an outcome or arriving at a desired destination?

Session and Circle Nine: Shouldville (Stay Far Away)

Oh, I could write a whole book on the soul sucking power of living in "Shouldville". You've seen this movie before, energy spent doing, thinking, worrying, operating the way others think you should or ought to no matter how much it erodes what you truly want, need or desire.

Don't pretend you don't know what I'm talking about! We've all called this place home. I ought to do this because others think it's right. I should do this because other people expect me to. Oh, I know, we must occasionally do things others or society expect of us but if we spend our entire lives in Shouldville, we run the risk of waking up one day only to realize we've done everything for others and nothing truly important for ourselves. This is a recipe for guilt, shame, anger, frustration, hopelessness but most of all, a significant blow to the confidence we have in ourselves.

I have coached women who grieved giving up their career and self-identity when they chose or were expected to take care of the home and or the kids. I've worked with others, men and women who desired different lives but needed to ensure their families were taken care of, so they went to work every day at a job that was lack luster but provided financial stability. I've spent countless hours with individuals who struggle with choosing a career path because of the pressure others (parents, friends, family, counselors) put on them, "suggesting" what they should do and others who are remorseful because they listened to those people and not their heart.

Here is a simple but profound truth. What you think you should do and what you need and or even love to do are often not the same. Here are some important questions to consider:

What things am I doing or thinking because I was told I should?

How much time do I spend doing things out of obligation/regret/guilt?

How would I feel if I spent more time on things I want to do or need to do as opposed to those I feel I should do?

What would I struggle to let go of?

What would I gain or benefit from if I did let those shoulds go?

Session and Circle Ten: Strengths & Gifts

Understanding your strengths and gifts is one of the most important outcomes of any coaching process. However, it is also critical to examine whether you truly enjoy your strengths or the things you are good at. As an example, I am exceptional at doing detailed type of work. I will tell you that most of the time I hate it! Just because you are great at something doesn't mean you love it or should be spending any serious amount of time doing it. As you go through the review of your answers in this session regarding strengths, ask if you like using these gifts. Here are some additional thoughtful questions to consider:

In what way does the world need the gifts I bring?

Which roles do I feel are best suited to my core strengths?

Where am I most effective, efficient, and productive?

What valuable strengths have I experienced throughout life that I want to share?

Where can I begin to share both what I am good at and enjoy?

Session and Circle Eleven: Contribution

I know you are here because you desire to live your best life! If someone hasn't told you lately you are extraordinary, and the world needs extraordinary. It needs you. All of you. The unique, fabulous, and best version of you!

Some time ago, I found myself engulfed in an intense identity crisis, the kind that completely knocks you off your feet and onto your you know what. Daily, I ended up choosing, almost reflexively yet consciously, to stay in a relationship that diminished me. I discovered the person I had been with for a decade and trusted completely was unfaithful. At my very core, I sensed and saw the warning signs that were there, but I chose to look away. It became seemingly easier to just fade into the background, into a shell of existence rather than face the truth. I sacrificed my peace of mind for the sake of stability.

Simultaneously, my work life wasn't much better. I worked for someone so difficult that no sane person would ever wish them to be their boss. When I tried to address their unprofessional behavior, the work environment turned retaliatory and toxic in nature, leading to daily migraines and a profound sense of despair. These were the physical manifestations of my denial, the price I was paying for not walking away.

Despite the adversity of personal and professional chaos, I took pride in my resilience, convincing myself that enduring silently was a sign of strength and not a symptom of my fear of failure or change. I revered my values of responsibility and determination, so I stubbornly resisted the changes necessary for my mental health, joy, and freedom.

Life sometimes hints, nudges, or even pushes you towards realizations. For me, it required a forceful outright shove, a clear signal that things were about to drastically be upended unless I paid attention.

Life had patiently waited for me to stop making excuses, but it couldn't wait forever. After enduring a year that tested the limits of my resilience, I arrived at a pivotal moment where the only way forward was out. The life I had known had become intolerable, a mere shadow of what it could be. It was time to wipe the slate clean and start anew, to embark on a courageous journey of profound reinvention. Let's be honest, it was one of the scariest times of my life, riddled with anxiety, indecision, and a wicked dose of self-doubt and personal self-sabotage.

I've learned and yet will continue to be profoundly grateful for paths not taken and wishes unfulfilled. The universe, in its myriad of ways is always guiding us, conspiring for us—if only we choose to notice and engage with it. It's no coincidence you're reading this; it's an invitation to explore and discover your soul's fingerprints upon your heart and to create a life that not only fulfills you but also brings joy to others.

.

NOW WHAT?

THE 5 KEY PRINCIPLES

Many people ask me, "what should I do with my life or for a living?" I do wish I held that crystal ball! Unfortunately, I don't have that superpower, but you are in luck, I know who does! Those answers are within you. My goal in sharing this process is to help unearth what you care most about so you can recognize opportunities when they walk by you. Remember the example where I asked you to look for every white car on the road? Clarity in what you are looking for creates a focus that helps and allows you to find it.

In the 15+ years I've been coaching folks, I've learned 5 key principles of creating the career and life you desire and deserve.

1. **Life is not a "to do list" nor an "I want to get list". It is being clear about:**

- How do you want to feel?

- What do you want to experience in life?

- What do you desire to contribute?

- Why do you want or care about these things you say you want?

- What's the next logical step that will lead you intentionally in that direction?

2. Avoid "how" questions (at least at first).

Figuring out the "how" can be a momentum and motivation killer and yet where do we often begin any effort? How will I achieve that? How will I do that? How is that possible? If we have clarity in our desires and an unbreakable conviction as to why it matters, the how will often find a way to manifest itself. How will come when you are clear about what and why.

3. Happiness is a mindset. Don't wait to be happy.

We are taught that success and contentment is dependent on what we achieve or receive. Happiness is therefore dependent on the result of something outside us, so we endlessly and often mindlessly chase the perfect life, love, job, car, house, kids (you get the drift). "When I find the love of my life, I will be happy!" "That car is amazing! I'm going to look killer in it!" "Children are the key to my happiness and all I need."

Giving top priority to achieving external happiness alters the nature of the questions we ask.

- What job do I want, or can I get vs. what work aligns with my gifts and how I can contribute?

- How much money will it pay vs. will it give me the opportunity to grow?

- How can I convince them I'm the right person for the job vs. is this the right opportunity for me?

I have met countless people who have everything, and they are miserable. They have traded in hours of their life for a stockpile of stuff they don't really need to impress people that they do not care about or even matter to them. The relentless pursuit of **more** results in a level of unconscious living, fleeting joy, and brief episodes of happiness. The antecedent is in the pause.

Give yourself a hand! You have now paused long enough to answer and perhaps raise new questions that define your version of happiness.

- What do I really want? I mean really want and why?

- Is how I want to feel available to me already without having to achieve a thing?

- What do I want to experience in this life? Why does that matter to me?

- What do I want to share or give?

- What do I want to be known for/stand for/contribute?

Why wait for happiness? It's yours right now.

4. The quality of your life is determined by the quality of questions you ask yourself.

Ask different kinds of questions, get a different quality of answers. Different answers lead to the creation of different stories or mental models. New feelings come from new mental models and a transformed future is the outcome.

5. Confidence is built in motion.

You've got this! With your talent, resilience, courage, and strength, you possess everything you need to create your extraordinary life! Simply step onto the playing field and take your first step (ok, or leap) towards your wishes, dreams, and passions, and then, take another. Confidence is built and strengthened through action/motion. Unfortunately, you can't think or worry yourself to success. Massive action consistently over time breeds results.

BONUS ROUND: THE BIG HAIRY QUESTIONS

Yes, there are just a few more! I promise this is it!

What would you regret most if you simply played it safe and didn't work towards your goals and dreams?

What will you need to unlearn to personally grow?

If you achieve your career goals, do you think you will feel the way you want to feel?

Are your current choices helping you build an inspiring future?

What can you feel today that doesn't require you to do anything except try it on and be it?

What's one step you will take to move in your heart's direction? What's the next one?

You are now 90 years old, sitting on a rocking chair outside your porch; you can feel the spring breeze gently brushing against your face. You are blissful and happy, pleased with the wonderful life you've been blessed to live. Looking back, what has mattered most to you? What are you most proud of? List them out.

There's one last exercise designed to help bring this all together. Think of it as your own personal mission statement or your own North Star. You've done the work, now this should be a sinch to complete.

My North Star

I will use my gifts and strengths of (*the gifts and strengths you uncovered*):

to (*what do you want to give, how do you want to contribute to the world*):

and through (*your most important values*):

I will (*legacy you want to leave or ultimate goal you would like to accomplish*):

Here is my example:

I will use my gifts of "seeing" and inspiring people, teaching, and caring for others to spark a change/lift/shift in people's thinking-from merely surviving to thriving; from settling for an ordinary life experience to creating and living an extraordinary one and through this passion and commitment of service to others I will humbly create and live an extraordinary life of my own.

Once you've written your statement, try it on. How does it feel? Take some time to sit with it and tweak it till it feels right. Do a couple versions and see which you gravitate towards or resonate the most with. When it feels right your version should feel congruent with who you think you are or desire to be. It should ring true for you; feel like coming home. When you read it aloud it may make you feel challenged or anxious, especially if it doesn't represent your current life. These are all natural reactions.

Over time, your life and needs evolve. You may want to revisit this exercise from time to time to refine and redefine your North Star. A career and a life are not destinations but journeys! There's some additional space to try a few options on should you need them.

My North Star: Take Two

I will use my gifts and strengths of (*the gifts and strengths you uncovered*):

to (*what do you want to give, how do you want to contribute to the world*):

and through (*your most important values*):

I will (*legacy you want to leave or ultimate goal you would like to accomplish*):

>>>⟶⟶

I will use my gifts and strengths of (*the gifts and strengths you uncovered*):

to (*what do you want to give, how do you want to contribute to the world*):

and through (*your most important values*):

I will (*legacy you want to leave or ultimate goal you would like to accomplish*):

What parts of your North Star statements feel "right" to you?

Which parts do you most resonate with?

What words don't add value to your statement that you could take out or replace?

WHAT NEXT?

"What next" you may be asking? First, pat yourself on the back, you have successfully answered over one hundred questions and taken a hard introspective look at your answers. Second, now you have a version of your North Star vision that feels authentic to you, keep it handy. It may sound funny but read it daily. Get familiar with it. It is now your new best friend! Where I find most people struggling is they are crystal clear about what they don't want but lack the clarity and conviction to find and work towards what they do want.

If you are looking for a profession or new profession options, I recommend my clients start exploring occupations that support their North Star vision. As an example, you have a list of skills, gifts, and strengths from answering these questions. You can make a top 10 list of those and enter them into a skills matcher software tool like the one sponsored by the U.S. Department of Labor below and see what jobs are recommended given your skill set.

https://www.careeronestop.org/Toolkit/Skills/skills-matcher.aspx

Once you identify a career that sounds interesting, read up on the profession. There are many websites online that can assist you with this research. You can find more resources on the Thrive Tribe Facebook page.

Social media networks and sites like LinkedIn offer you an opportunity to create a profile and meet other people who may be doing what you want to do. I know it may sound scary, but reaching out to someone, even someone you don't know who does the work you are interested in is often the best way to get firsthand information about what life is really like for them in that role or business.

 As you go about your search here are some key questions to ask yourself, using your North Star Vision as a guide.

- Does the role/job description/business opportunity sound like it supports my North Star vision?

- What is it about that role or opportunity that sounds interesting or intriguing to me?

- What parts of it am I attracted to and why? Do they align with how I want to contribute to the world?

- What organizations hire roles like this?

- Do the values of the business or organization match my values or seem like they would be a good match to leverage my gifts?

- Would I be able to believe in the work that I'm doing and how I'm contributing?

- Does this type of work allow me to live the life I desire to live in the way I want to show up and live it?

- Who could I find that does this work or runs this type of business?

- What would I like to learn from them to gain enough information and understanding to feel a level of confidence in my direction?

There is a phrase you will hear if you spend any time in the London subway system, "Please Mind the Gap". Even though the phrase is used to warn travelers of the gap between the station and the train, I often think it's useful in terms of thinking about our lives. For most of us, there will always be a gap between who we are and who we desire to be. Too often we spend time thinking about who we've been (past) and who we would like to be (future) that we swing from one or circle around one and then back to the other without taking the time to pause and truly listen to what the current moment is offering and sharing with us.

Yes, admittedly the questions you have been answering have been designed to help you explore two of the three dimensions to define the gap, but now that we've done that it comes down to what steps can we take in the now to mind the gap?

COMMITMENT TO SEEKING

Every summer my family and I would make the trek out to see my grandparents in a small urban Colorado town. Routinely we would end our enjoyable, relaxing picnic by the creek with a lengthy hike up some mountain trail. It wasn't that I didn't enjoy hiking, it's just that my legs would get tired. After all, my daily walk to school was in flat land country! My grandfather, who somehow knew I was getting tired despite my lack of complaint, would always tell me at the perfect moment "Just put one foot in front of the other." Sage advice.

Thinking about starting something new, beginning again, starting over, quitting, moving on, changing directions isn't without angst and perhaps a healthy level of anxiousness. My grandfather was right though, the journey always starts with the first step and then another and another. Don't let the destination scare you. You can do the little stuff until it collectively becomes the big stuff.

When I get stuck in my fears or in my head, I find this question to be most helpful. What's the next right or logical step? What could these collective steps mean 5 years from now?

Let's look at that for you. Now that you have taken the time to go through this question journey what is the next logical step?

What is the next thing you can do or action you can take to move in the direction you desire to go?

What's the next thing…

…and the next?

Who can help me? (Hint: Thrive Tribe Community) If I don't know anyone personally could I meet them through someone else or somewhere else?

What is one shift in perspective that I need to support my journey?

How has life been preparing me for this exact moment?

What am I committed to doing today? Do it or calendar it!

How am I going to show up today for myself and what I am committing to?

How will I feel differently if I just take the next right step?

Build a plan before you start every new day that focuses on the next one or two logical and meaningful steps. You don't have to build a big Taj Mahal, my friends, but you must build meaningful and progressive action into each day. Don't overcomplicate it. You've got this!

What meaningful action(s) will I take today?

How will I feel when I complete it?

ONE MORE THING

"The Meaning of Life is to Find Your Gift. The Purpose of Life is to Give It Away."

--Pablo Picasso

I am sincerely grateful you have come this far and that you've given me an opportunity to be your guide. My hope had always been that this book would find its way to the seeker with the intention of being what one needed, exactly when it was needed most.

I wasn't kidding when I said there will never be another you! The questions, but most importantly your answers, hopefully served as a spark, a reminder of your significance. So, cheers to you! Your best life awaits!

Let's get to it!

A SPECIAL FAVOR & SURPRISE!

Hello, my dear friends! I have a **small humble ask**; if you found **value** in the book and the free companion course, please consider **sharing your experience with a positive star rating** and or written review **on Amazon.**

My goal is to add as much value and help as I possibly can. It's always best to have help along the road of discovery. The only way this help gets in the hands of those who need it **is if they see it.** The hard truth: the more positive reviews—the more the book gets seen. I am sincerely **grateful** to you in advance!

🎁 Here's a surprise you probably weren't expecting, **the *NOW WHAT?* Companion Course!** As a gift for purchasing this book, you now have **lifetime access** to an exclusive course designed to take your experience to the next level. Inside, you'll find:

- **Interactive exercises** that align with the book's chapters, helping you apply what you're learning.
- **Lessons** with actionable tips and insights to fuel your progress.
- **Practical tools and templates** to help you stay organized and focused.
- **Ongoing inspiration** to keep you moving forward, no matter what challenges arise.

This course was created with YOU in mind—a supportive, hands-on companion to ensure you're not just reading but *transforming*.   https://o2xolife.uteach.io

I can't wait to see what you uncover, create, and achieve. Let's make "What's next?" your greatest adventure yet!

Best wishes,

JOIN OUR THRIVE TRIBE COMMUNITY

Are you eager to elevate or enhance your professional and personal journey but hesitant to do it on your own? Looking for a comprehensive resource hub? If that's the case, the Thrive Tribe Facebook group is the perfect place for you. This group is a private space dedicated to those who have purchased this book. Join to access exclusive content, motivational insights, informative articles, and thought-provoking questions designed to transform your life. Simply visit the link or scan the QR Code, answer a brief questionnaire, and enter your book order number to get started! This community provides exclusively free content and support for owners and operators of this book.   Think of it as a book bonus!
https://www.facebook.com/groups/698917771615681/

A BIT ABOUT THE AUTHOR

Angie VanArsdale is more than her titles of author, speaker, consultant, and professional coach; she embodies a dynamic fusion of energy, expertise, and empathy guiding individuals and organizations on transformative journeys to their definition of success. As founder of VanArsdale Consulting Group and O2XO, her focus is deeply rooted in the belief that everyone can achieve remarkable growth and breakthroughs. Angie's approach is rich in actionable insight, tailored to unleash and unlock the inherent strengths within each person, turning every engagement into a catalyst for positive change. Her life's mission reflects her belief in the potential of every individual and organization to achieve extraordinary things!

Boy, that sounds very official! I'm also a proud dog mom, a lover of travel and taking pictures of everything, hanging out on my back porch, messing about in the garden, sitting still for hours watching my bees, hunting for treasures along any seashore, and watching the sun go down with a beverage in hand!

CONNECT WITH US!

Email: o2xolife@gmail.com

Website: o2xolife.uteach.io

  https://www.facebook.com/o2xolife

  https://www.instagram.com/ordinarytoxtraordinary/

Made in United States
Troutdale, OR
04/06/2025